Graced For It

Walk In Purpose, Live In Peace

Chantea M. Williams

Graced For It
Copyright © 2020 by Chantea M. Williams.

All rights reserved. Printed in the United States of America. No part of this book may be used or reproduced in any manner whatsoever without written permission except in the case of brief quotations em- bodied in critical articles or reviews.

Published by :
Relentless Publishing House
www.relentlesspublishing.com

Ordering Information :
Quantity sales and special discounts are available. For details, contant Publisher at info@relentlesspublishing.com.

ISBN:978-1-948829-72-4 (Hardback)
ISBN : 978-1-948829-83-0 (Ebook)

Table of Contents

Introduction	1
Self-Care	5
Reset and Refocus	13
What Is Your Vision?	23
Believe Is Yourself	31
Get Back Up	39
Walk It Out	47
There Is Still Room	55
You Always Had Victory	61
Who's In Your Situation Room?	67
You Are Not Forgotten	75
It's Already Yours	81
Will You Chase Purpose?	91
You Are Graced for the Assignment	97
About the Author	101

INTRODUCTION

Are you sabotaging your own greatness?

Do you know exactly what you are created to do? Have you tapped into your Kingdom assignment in the earth? I had to OVERCOME me before I could do anything that God had already purposed me to do. I had so much low self-esteem, self-doubt, negative mindset, people pleasing demeanor and tunnel vision. I couldn't fathom the thought of God actually having anything great for me to do. After all, why would He want someone like me to do anything more than what I was doing? Surly He couldn't use a former teen mom. I wasn't anybody special. I had no special gifts or talents so I thought. For years I suffered silently with depression and accepted a plethora of things that anybody threw my way when I should have thrown it right back at them. I was my worst enemy and didn't even know it. Can you relate to any of these things?

To be very frank, my life didn't start changing until I was around people whose mindset was direct opposite of mine. Only then did I see just how screwed up I was and how miserable I was making my own life. As I look back over my life in reflection, I see how I allowed too many people to take advantage of me. All because I didn't know who I was and not being confident within myself beyond being a good mother. There were many days I felt I couldn't even do that right. I was so caught up in providing a good life for my child and proving to the naysayers that I didn't mess my life up after all. The good news is that I slowly, but surely came out of that slump and there was no turning back. The more I was introduced to greater the more I began to believe that there was greater for my life. The more chances I took on me the more I wanted to take. As my thoughts changed about myself, my actions began to follow. I became more confident and bolder. I desired to reach for the stars even if it meant I would miss it from time to time. I had resolved within myself that **Giving Up Was Never An Option** again!

Overcoming myself was not an easy task. I had to confront the ugly side of me and admit that I have not treated myself well. I had to conquer me in order to live. Think about that statement for a minute. I had to retrain my mind to think well of myself and seek out God's purpose for my life. Even while on that journey, I still had doubts as to whether or not I was capable of doing any of it. Honestly, there are days I still fight that battle. Not so much that I don't believe, but because that old me tries to resurrect and sabotage my purpose. I am able to recognize it more quickly and immediately cast those thoughts down. If I'm having a slow day, I have surrounded myself with people who speak life into me and pray over me. I have chosen to continually do the work of conquering me so that I can be the Greater Working Woman He has already created me to be. I will fight for me!

It feels good to no longer have the burden of trying to please people who will never be pleased. I wake up every morning with a drive to pursue my purpose and some days it's by any means necessary. This book is a testament of my 40 years of life and counting. I'm sharing with you the wisdom I gained when finding and believing that I am Graced For It. There are so many life lessons I have learned about just me and I'm sharing with you a few of them in this book. The foundation of Graced For It is the book of Esther. A little Hebrew girl who had no desire to ever be queen was placed in the palace, found favor with everyone and received the crown. She had help along the way to reveal to her the very thing she was graced to do. Her obedience to her purpose saved an entire nation. It is my heart, that every woman and man (wink) is GRACED to do something. It is your responsibility to find out what that something is. As you read the pages of this book, I encourage you to answer the questions at the end of each chapter to help guide you and/or remind you of your purpose in life. I would love to know how this book has assisted you on your purpose journey. Feel free to email me to share your insights info@greaterwomen.com.

Chantea M. Williams

Self-Care

How well do you treat you?

Self-care is care provided for you and by you. It's about identifying your own needs and taking steps to meet them. It is taking the time to do some of the activities that nurture you. Self-care is about taking proper care of yourself and treating yourself as kindly as you treat others. Self-care is not selfish. It's necessary. Are you living life like its golden and what does that mean to you? (This is one of my favorite Jill Scott songs.)

We all have different things that makes our life enjoyable, but are you making time to do those things? You know, for me, living life like its golden is on the beach, looking at the waves and reading a good book. Sometimes it's in the kitchen while baking and I don't care about anything else. Like that's my happy space. That's my stress-free space. I know that sounds crazy, right? But that's me. Those things make my life golden. Just having the freedom. As women, we do a lot of things for a lot of people. We take care of everybody but ourselves. Think about it. When was the last time you took some "me" time and you didn't feel guilty? When was the last time you said, "You know what, I love y'all, but I'm taking me a minute?" When was the last time you cared more about you without feeling guilty or the need to provide an explanation? It's okay to be selfish from time to time and do something that you really enjoy. When was the last time you just hung out with your girlfriends and you all laughed for no particular reason at all? You know that belly roll laugh, where you got to be like, wait a minute, I'm going to pee on myself and you just had fun.

A lot of us are so busy taking care of things, doing this, doing that, and doing whatever. We are existing through life and we're not living through life. What does it take for you to live your life like its golden? For those of us that are church girls, it doesn't have to be about church? I love church. I love ministry. However, that's not living my golden life. Church is not always fun. Its work and a lot of it. You may need to take a Sunday off and just chill. Let the right people know so that others can be in place. It's okay! It doesn't mean you left the church or that you left God. Some of us are so involved in ministry that it is has become our whole life! We have been made to feel guilty if we decide to take a break. We have Martha moments- busy and worried about many things and not taking care of ourselves in the process. We wait until we shut down or get sat down and it shouldn't be that way. Life is short and you need to live it like its golden every single day. No regrets. No woulda, shoulda and couldas. Nope, it's not allowed. I challenge you to intentionally make time for you. Schedule your self-care like you do hair and doctor's appointments. If you're not good and you're not healthy, how can you be there for anybody else?

    I remember, as I was getting more active in church, I planned my entire life around all the church activities so I could be there. I was my pastor's assistant, which also meant I was over the administrative ministry. I was a youth Sunday school teacher, intercessory prayer ministry, youth bible study teacher, VBS teacher and coordinator, kitchen ministry and whatever else needed to get done. I slowly stepped down from a few things but I would soon pick something else up. I don't know about you, but I just got tired typing all that. I remember telling my mother that I couldn't do something because I had to be at church and she told me, "Chantea, that church will go on if you die tomorrow." She knew everything I did for the church. I was a single mother and trying my best to live for the Lord, but I was going about it the wrong way.

Things were being done but I wasn't taking care of myself like I should. No one should be that involved in ministry! That is not the abundant life that Jesus died for. Even the airlines know the importance of self-care. When the flight attendant is giving instructions before takeoff, they express the importance of putting on your own oxygen mask before being able to help anyone else. It has become the norm for many people and especially women to put on everyone else's oxygen masks before they even think about their own. Think about the danger in that and the changes you need to make in your own life today.

Here are some tips to get you started with your self-care:

1. **Schedule your self-care time every week:** You may not do the same thing every week, but you need at least 30 minutes to 1 hour of uninterrupted quiet time.

2. **Get a massage:** Schedule one at least once a month.

3. **Exercise:** taking care of your body is the ultimate self-care. You only get once chance to use it. Make it count.

4. **Spend time with your girl friends:** Don't neglect your friends because you wear a collar. You should go see a movie, brunch or dessert.

5. **Take a vacation:** You need a mini break even if it's only for a weekend.

6. **Take a hot bath:** Soaking in the tub relaxes your muscles. Turn on same jazz, light you a candle and enjoy.

7. **Start a hobby:** Whether it's planting a garden, painting, crafting, etc. Do something outside of ministry. Something that will relax you.

8. **Sabbath:** Make sure you have one day a week that you just rest and meditate. If God rested after creating the world in six days, surely we can take one day to rest.

9. **Sabbatical:** You need a longer length of time to refresh yourself. Spend time with God to make sure you are still in alignment with His purpose for your life. Get away from everyone and everything. Your ministry will thank you for it.

As women it can sometimes be challenging to think of ourselves before others. There are no "superwomans." She is a myth. You don't have to be all over the place to prove anything. When you allow others to monopolize your time, you are teaching them that you don't matter. We teach people how to treat us based on how we treat ourselves.

How have you been treating yourself lately?

When was the last time you got 6-8 hours of sleep?

When was the last time you did something for yourself that wasn't initiated by someone else?

Has anyone ever asked you what does your self-care look like?

Take a moment to ask yourself, "What have I done for me lately?"

Sit down and write out things that you like to do that you haven't done in a long time. It doesn't matter how silly it is. That's what living the golden life is all about. It doesn't matter what anybody thinks about it. It's what you want to do. Make it your new priority to take better care of you starting right now!

How are you going to take care of you?

Reset and Refocus

It's okay to start over again.

It is time to refocus and reset. You can push that reset button and start all over again. Yes, it may take time. Yes, may be inconvenient. Yes, it may not feel good or look good. You may be all out of sorts, off track or may have even given up. You may have people looking at you crazy saying, "What in the world are you doing?" Refocus and reset yourself and get back on track. It's not too late. It's not over. Don't make any excuses.

I want you to reset your thinking. I want you to reset the words that are coming out of your mouth and over yourself. Stop repeating what people said about you. Just because they said it doesn't make it your truth, but the moment you start declaring it over your life, it becomes your reality. So, let me ask you, "How is that working for you?"

How are those negative opinions working for you? How is the rumor that you keep replaying over and over and over in your head working for you? How is that mistake you wish you never made, that you have chosen to not get over, working out for you? Take some time and sit in quiet place and meditate. Ask God for strategic instructions on what you need to do to get back on track; then actually follow those instructions, and be obedient to everything He tells you to do.

Don't give up, give IT up. Don't give up, give IT up. I watched a message by Dr. Dharius Daniel and when he made that statement in his message, it absolutely just captivated me. I just had to pause and think how many times I gave up? I know a lot of us have started things and stopped multiple times because it didn't work out the way we wanted. We automatically assumed, "Oh well it's not my time." "It's not for me." "It's too difficult." "It's too hard." "You know, I look foolish." "I feel like I'm failing." Listen, you gave up too soon. You tried to do it in your own strength. You tried to do it in your own knowledge. You tried to do it your own way. It's not going to work that way. You have to give it up to God. You have to ask Him.

Proverbs 16:3

"Commit your plans to the Lord so that they shall succeed."

We aren't succeeding because we're not committing our plans to God which in return may cause us to give up instead of giving it up. A lot of us started a business and it didn't work out and we gave up and said, well, I'm never doing that again, but did you take your business to God consistently? Did you ask Him, "God, tell me how I'm supposed to do this? You are the CEO. Tell me where I was supposed to go. Tell me what product and services to offer." No, you did something that you thought was right. You got your head pumped up by family and friends and says, oh, you'll do good, but when you fail, you gave up. Listen, some of you want to go back to school, but life happened. You went into a withdrawal period and you said, "Well that time has passed." You gave up and you didn't give it up, right? You may have had a failed relationship and said, "Oh, well I'm never going to fall in love again because I don't want my heart to get broken." You gave up and you didn't give it up. We put our faith and trust in ourselves, people and in things, when we should be putting it in God. The reason why you're giving up is because you won't give it up. Let me ask you, what is the IT that you need to give up instead of giving up on the IT?

Just because it failed doesn't mean you weren't supposed to do it. Just because it didn't work out doesn't mean that it wasn't for you. Sometimes our timing is wrong. Sometimes we get so ambitious and just so anxious that we move ahead of God. The circumstances weren't right. The ground wasn't right. The people may not have been ready. It doesn't always mean that it wasn't what you were suppose to do. Go dig again. There's a story in the book of Genesis where Isaac was digging the wells that his father had dug and every time he dug a well, the people of the land contended with him and said this is our well. He kept digging it until he got to a well that he didn't have to contend with anyone. He called that place *Rehoboth*, which means *God made room for me*.

God has already made room for you, but He's waiting for you to give it up instead of giving God. Beloved, stop giving up so soon. Stop giving up when it gets hard. Stop giving up when you get your heart broke. Stop giving up because it didn't work out the way you wanted it. Stop giving up because certain people aren't supporting you. Stop giving up because you're doing it in your own strength and instead of giving up, give it up, right? Make the declaration, "I'm going to give it up and not give up!" Do you know that giving up is never an option when you have already been created for greatness? God has anointed you for a specific kingdom purpose- this is your assignment.

You still have time to get it right. You still have time to start over. You still have time to get it accomplished. You still have time. Get refocused so the rest of your life can be about purpose. Stop complaining. Change your perspective on what it is and look at it differently. Stop beating yourself up. Stop entertaining negative thoughts and get yourself refocused. Stop wasting time on worrying about how you got off track. That does not matter. The point is for you to realize you got off track and make the necessary adjustments to get back on track, because purpose is waiting. Giving up is never an option.

People that are assigned to you, are waiting. They're waiting for you to show up and show out. They're waiting for you to be in position so that they can get what they need. They're waiting for you to do what you've been called and anointed to do so that they can be blessed. Your blessings are tied into your refocusing. It's tied into your obedience. It's tied into walking in your purpose. It's tied to you being faithful. Don't allow the enemy to torture you in your mind. **God already knew you would be here and He didn't change His mind or His plans for your life.** Read that last sentence again.

You may need to slow down and stop doing so much. Are you a busy body? Stop assuming you have to be everywhere all the time. There are some engagements you probably need to cancel because it's busy time and it's distracting you from your purpose. Yeah. You need to go back and say, "You know what? I can't go because I need to get refocused. I need to be about my business. I need to be walking in purpose. I need to be doing the things that I know I'm supposed to be doing." It's time to get back refocused.

I don't care how you feel. Don't give up. I don't care how many times you've messed up doing the same thing. Don't give up. It's time to reset and refocus. You can still accomplish that goal. You can still accomplish that dream. You may have to let go of some things and some people. In order for you to be successful, it's going to sit down in some quiet time and get some clarity.

We get off focus because we didn't commit anything to God. We made plans, but we didn't ask Him what was His plan or His opinion on the matter. We just went with it because it made sense. It's time to walk in purpose so that we can live in peace. It's time to walk in purpose so that we can have victory. It's time to walk in purpose so we can have that abundant life that we claim and shout about. Some of us are miserable because we haven't press the reset button and we haven't refocused. That may be the reason why you're frustrated. The reason why it feels like you're spinning your wheels like a hamster because you are doing the same thing, yet praying for a different result.

Sit down somewhere, literally, and refocus. When I feel like that and when I have so much going on or feel like I'm being pulled to the left or right, I sit in a quiet place and play instrumental music. I meditate and ask God:

1. *Show me how to do what You have already told me to do.*
2. *What do I need to eliminate?*
3. *Show me how to get back on track.*

If you want to be successful in life, you must rest and refocus. If your business isn't going right, ask yourself, is it God's plan or is that my plan? If your ministry seems out of sorts, are you doing what He told you to do or are you doing what's popular?

You probably already know what areas of your life you need to reset and refocus. The choice is still yours. We all have to do it from time to time. There's no shame in it. You cannot walk in what God has already graced you to do if your life and your spirit are in total chaos. It's time to get them both together.

How are you going to reset and refocus?

Doing the same thing will never get you new results. You must assess what is and what is not working in order to make the necessary adjustments.

~ CMW

What Is Your Vision?

You must see it before you see it.

I've seen so many people, just all over the place and they're not settled. They are just a busy body. Wanting to be doing something versus nothing, but not willing to do the work to figure out what it is they're actually suppose to be doing. I want you to settle down and ask yourself, "What was I created to do?" It may be what you do naturally. That thing that you're always thinking about, but keep talking yourself out of doing. On the other hand, you have people who say they want to do something, but don't have the drive to get it done. They could be fearful, lack of resources, their environment, comparing themselves to others, laziness or even procrastination.

If you have something that you want to do, and haven't made steps toward to getting that done, then my question becomes, "Do you really want it?" I remember coming up and just trying to figure this whole thing out about who I am and my purpose. My drive was my need to prove people wrong. I became a mom at 15 and that in itself was a huge obstacle, a lot of statistics, negative feedback and opinions and not to mention the things that I was battling with internally. My whole thing was to prove to people that I didn't screw my life up. For a number of years, that was my drive. As I started to seek my purpose, my drive shifted from trying to prove something to people and even myself, to pursuing my purpose. I had to stop comparing myself and let go of the fear of being a failure. I couldn't allow the lack of resources to stop me. I had to decide whether or not I was going to do what I felt like I was created to do.

There comes a time in our lives that we have to ask ourselves the question, "Do I want to do what I've been put on this earth to do?" Because the matter of the fact is we all can make an excuse and even justify it. Get a little compassion and sympathy from other people, but at the end of the day, I'm just a firm believer with everything in my heart, if you believe that you're supposed to do something, then you're going to get up and do it. As the old saying goes, where there's a will, there's a way. If there's nothing driving you, then are your goals, really your goals?

People always say this, "What would you do if you didn't have to worry about money? What would you do and not get paid for?" Start right there. Your purpose and your vision have nothing to do with the amount of money in your bank account. Nothing to do with your connections. Nothing to do with the size of your platform, the number of your followers, but it has everything to do with the anointing that's already on your life. That is priceless. You cannot buy it or sell it. Your purpose does not come from people. Our purpose does not come from laying on hands or a prophecy. Our purpose was already given to us before the foundation of the world. God has given every one of His children a distinct purpose. Your purpose is not going to be like anybody else's. Their journey may look similar. You may go through similar trial or even have similar successes, but your purpose is unique to you. Once you find out your purpose, then you get a vision. What is the vision for your life? Not what is in your head. What are you willing to write down in order to hold yourself accountable? What are you willing to share with somebody so that they could hold you accountable? Some people are vision killers. Use wisdom and discernment with those who you share your vision and purpose. You do not need people to kill what you got going on before you even get started good.

I made a choice to put three white boards in my dining room and I have written down personal, business and ministry goals. Let me be very transparent. It is the absolute first time I actually wrote it down in a public place so that when somebody comes over, they see it, which means they can ask about it. I want to challenge you. Write your vision down and if you don't have a white board, write it on the sheet of paper and then stick it on the wall and hold yourself accountable. Every day you need to look at it and say, okay, what am I doing to get here? I know some of us dream big and God can do all things. I'm not doubting your faith. I'm imploring you to use wisdom. There's nothing wrong with dreaming big, but ask yourself, is it realistic? A vision will always be tested by tribulations. Faithfulness to vision is one of the marks of its legitimacy. A lot of us will leave our vision the time it gets hard. The moment things don't look like the way we thought or when nobody supports it, the first thing we say is, oh, well, I don't think I need to be doing this. That is not a measurement of whether or not you missed the mark. I have hosted webinars whether people signed up or not. I still got on the webinar and taught the session. Why? Because I was faithful to the vision and the call I knew God had directed me. I didn't allow numbers to distract me. While numbers are good, it's not the tell all to determine the validity of your purpose or your vision. What did you walk away from because the numbers were not there? You know, we love to, to quote Habakkuk 2:3 but do you actually write the vision? Like literally not figuratively speaking. I mean, you write it on a piece of paper. We love to quote that verse, but we don't actually take the necessary action.

I'm telling you, since I have been more disciplined and focused and intentional on the vision and purpose that God has for my life, I have been more successful and prosperous in all things. It's imperative that you hold fast to your vision and don't let it go. Don't give up. Don't walk away from it because things don't line up or because somebody said something negative. You don't need another person to lay hands on you, to speak a prophecy over you or to affirm you. God has already affirmed you in Ephesians 2:10. He says that we are His workmanship created for good works. You are His masterpiece. Since you're already a masterpiece, why are you wanting another masterpiece to affirm you? You've already been affirmed by the Creator. Why do you need somebody else to speak your vision into fruition? It's already on the inside of you and it is your responsibility to stir it up. It's your responsibility to write it out and make it plain. That's your responsibility. Nobody else's. What are you going to do? Are you going to allow your vision to lay idle or are you going to get moving? The choice is yours. You have to be intentional. When you make a decision that you want for yourself, things will start to line up. But guess what? You gotta do the work. God has already done His part and now it's your turn to care.

What is the vision you see for your life?

Believe In Yourself

You are worth it.

You know, if we're honest, our faith isn't lit in every area of our life. Can you be honest and admit that sometimes you still struggle in your faith? The confidence that you possess sometimes fluctuates. It doesn't make you a bad person. It affirms your humanity. You are in company of Jesus' disciples because they also struggled. They walked with Jesus, having firsthand knowledge and a front row seat to the things He did and said. They still struggled in their faith. Take a deep breath. You're not alone.

Have you been praying, and still haven't received it? Many of you may want to believe the enemy is hindering your blessings, but the truth is the negative words that come out of your mouth may block your blessings. Death and life are in the power of the tongue. They that love it will eat the fruit thereof. If you're getting rotten fruit, you're probably speaking rotten words. Speak life! Even when it looks like death, speak life. Even when it smells like death, speak like. No matter what anybody else is saying or doing, you better speak life until you can touch it. You better speak a life until you can see it. You better speak life to everything He has promised you comes to pass. Don't allow what you see to dictate what you say, because what you say is what you will see. Did you catch what I said? Don't allow what you see to dictate what you say, because what you say is what you see.

It may look a little shaky. It may feel a little weird, but listen, if you're believing God for something, believe with all your heart. Every single day, water it with a little more faith than the day before. Faith is not idle. Your actions should be evidence of your faith. Do you continually tell yourself that you're not worthy to receive what you're asking God for? Let me let you in a little secret, you'll never be worthy. We will never be worthy. It is only because of the unmerited favor of God that we are who we are. It is by the grace of God I am who I am. You can go ahead and cut that excuse out right now. Is your negative thinking hindering your faith? However, we think will flow into our hearts and now we have a heart issue. Your heart is a reflection of what's already been festering in your mind.

Here's another thing I found out that could be hindering your prayers, your circle of friends. What is your circle saying on a regular basis? Their faith is not needed for you to get what you need. Let me help free you. Their faith is not needed for you to get what you need. It's all about your faith. Now I got some friends and we cut up really good. I mean, we just straight up have fun, but I also have friends who push and correct me into purpose. We hold each other accountable. What is your circle doing to help hinder or grow your faith? When was the last time you got on the phone with your friends talking about purpose and the plan God has for your individual lives, where you are now, where you should be, things you need to correct, things you need to let go and things you should be doing? Do you have those type of friends? If you don't check your circle. You need to ask yourself why not? Have I not connected with others who will stand in faith with me? I'm talking about the type of friends that will push you even though there is no benefit for them. I'm not talking about the friends who stay around because they know that they're going to get some of the blessings too. Do you have those types of friends? Don't let the people in your circle cause you to have shaky faith and speak doubt over what you prayed.

I know what it feels like when your faith has wavered

or to have people who you love and trust to shoot down the things that you feel that God is going to do for you. Then you tell yourself, well, maybe it's not for me. I know what it feels like to wait and wait for something and then think it probably wasn't for me. I wasn't good enough. God is not moved by time because He is time. Everything is in His divine timing. We get impatient because things don't happen right now. We don't serve a microwave God, and He doesn't give microwave blessings. He doesn't have a microwave purpose for your life. We cannot have microwave faith. That's not going to get you anywhere. Unless God has specifically told you no, it is still an open heaven. You still have access. It is time for us to level up our faith, make moves and stop the excuses. You'll never get it what's already yours, if you don't start increasing faith. It's time for you to really experience Ephesians 3:20. God has no respect of persons and because He has no respect of persons, you have access to Him just like everybody else. You need the faith and boldness to go to Him and say, *"God, I want everything that You have for me because You didn't change Your mind about me. I want to experience it all."* Are you really going to have more faith for others and not have that same level of faith for yourself? There are some things that God is waiting on you to do, because everything that's going to happen in your life, every blessing, has already been written in heaven. God is not trying to figure out how to bless you. He already knows it. He's already worked it out. He's waiting for you to get in alignment with Him. Are you ready to go all in?

God has given us all a measure of faith. Work your measure of faith, to the best of your ability. Stop comparing your measure to somebody else's measure. We all have different levels of faith. If you want more faith, read more word. Surround yourself with people who have big faith. Listen to how they talk and watch how they move. It's time for your faith to have mobility. Everywhere you go, your faith goes! It's time to graduate from mustard seed faith. Your faith needs to start producing a harvest!

Write down positive affirmations to speak over yourself and your purpose.

Until you find your purpose, others will find it for you.

~ CMW

Get Back Up

It's time to finish what you started

I have the privilege and the honor to host my Young Writers Academy, which is an online academy for young writers grades K through 12. I teach them how to write and they publish their book at the end of the academy. During my first one on one session with one of my writers, she was telling me about her book and went to go get the drawing of the book cover that she created. She went to go get it and couldn't find it. She says, "Well, it's not where I last put it. I guess my sister needed a sheet of paper because I can't find it, but that's okay. I'll just draw it again for you." This little young girl blessed my whole life. She commences to start drawing her book cover over again and it took her all of two minutes. She flipped it over and showed me. How many of us panic when things don't go right? How many of us spend too much time and energy talking about what went wrong instead of taking the steps to make it right again? The simple fact that this little girl didn't stop. She didn't cry. She didn't have a temper tantrum. She just said, "That's okay. I'll just draw you another one." If we would take that attitude, energy, and initiative to look at a situation and say, you know this is not going the way I thought it should. I'm not getting the results I want, but it is okay. I'm going to try again. The fact that this young writer didn't freak out or get mad at her little sister for moving her piece of paper, but instead she realized that what was in her was already in her. The fact that she couldn't find the paper didn't mean she couldn't duplicate it. Did you catch that?

    She realized that what was in her was still in her. There was no need for her to freak out. A lot of times, we freak out over things we don't have control over. Yes, it would have been great if her little sister didn't touch her stuff. It would have been great if her paper was where she left it. See, she understood I can duplicate it. I can do it again. If we would have that same attitude and say, you know what, maybe I planned this conference and it didn't happen the first time the way I wanted too. Guess what? The gifts are still in you. The vision is still in you. Do it again and make it work. Stop complaining about what didn't happen or go. Stop worrying about what you can't control. What's in you is in you. Just duplicate it and do it again. You understand what I'm saying? Stop having adult temper tantrums. Analyze it and keep it moving. I want to encourage you to try again. Plan that event again. Write that book again. Start that business over. Whatever didn't work, doesn't mean that you are a failure. It just means that it didn't work out. Go do it again because purpose is still in you. Don't lose faith because it didn't work. Get yourself together. Dry your tears and swallow your pride. Get back up and do it again. It's time for your comeback.

I don't care how many times you tried and failed. I don't care how many people have told you no. That's not excused. I don't care if you don't have the platform or the resources. I don't care if you don't have a big following, that's not an excuse. I don't have a big following. I don't have a super major platform and yet here you are reading my book. I'm not moved by numbers. I'm moved by my Kingdom assignment. I'm not moved by the opinions of people. I'm moved by the word of God. I'm moved by His instructions. I'm moved by His voice. It is time to get back up. I used to be there. I know what it feels like when you think you're not worthy. When you've tried to change you, but still mess up again. You will never live life like its golden unless you get back up again. The Bible says, a just man falls seven times and gets back up. After he failed the first time he could have stayed down, but he got back up. The second time he could have stayed down, but he got back up. He could have said, now wait a minute. I'm tired of falling, but he got back up the third, fourth, fifth, sixth, and seventh time. When teaching a child how to ride bike, they get a little wobbly at first. They may fall down several times before they get it right. We encourage them to keep trying because we know the joy and excitement that comes with riding a bike. It's the same thing in life. You're going to fall down. You're going to get scrapes and bruises. Things are going to hit you and hurt, but you got to get back up. You can't allow the excuse that, "Oh, I'm just feeling down, So-and-so did this to me. I went through this or I made a bad decision over here." Get back up! Whatever it is that has caused you to fall down and stay down. I want you to look at that thing and say, you know what? I'm getting back up. I may fall down again. I may mess up again. I may make another bad decision, but I choose not to stay down. I'm going to Get Back Up!

There is a story in the Bible where a father took his demon possessed son to some of the disciples and they couldn't heal him. When Jesus came down off the mountain, Jesus has a conversation with the father. The father asked, "Jesus, if you can heal, my son will you?" Jesus responded if and the father immediately said help my unbelief. Sometimes we just have to ask God, help our unbelief. A lot of us, we have self-doubt. We have that insecurity. We have those things on the inside of us that tells us now, you know, you can't do that. You know, if you put on that event, nobody's going to come. You know, if you write that book, nobody's going to buy it. You know, if you launched that business, nobody's going to support you. You know, if you open up that nonprofit, you're not going to have anybody to service. You know, if you do this, that's not going to work. We have all of those doubts on the inside of us that are telling us not to do it. Silence those voices by your actions. Time to get back up. No more excuses. No more living a subpar life. No more allowing your past to keep you arrested. No more allowing the opinions of other people to be your reality. It is time to get back up. Whatever you're facing or going through in your life, I want you to look that thing flat-footed in the face and tell it, "You're not going to keep me down any longer. I'm going to get back up now!"

How will you get back up?

Nothing and no one can keep you down unless you choose to be down.

~ CMW

Walk It Out

Someone Is Waiting On You

I started an anthology project for women who were young mothers to share their struggles and victories. Let me be very honest. I had been sitting on this project for about two years prior to starting it. When God first gave me the idea, I doubted myself. I told myself who are you to do such a project. You don't really know anybody. You don't have the platform. You don't have the influence. Who's really going to join it? I didn't do anything. I just put it on the back burner and let it go. As I became a part of an anthology project, that urge and desire was rekindled. I put it out there and with an investment fee because I didn't have the money to pay for it. Only two people signed up and paid. I'm praying and asking God what am I doing wrong? He said, I never told you to charge for this. God reminded me when He gives you the vision, He also makes the full provision. He literally checked me. I went back and started over. I took the investment fee off and refunded the other two women. After that, God blessed me with the most wonderful group of women. One of them posted how grateful they were to my obedience to this project because it rebirthed some projects that God had put on the inside of her. My heart was so overjoyed when I read that. You never know who is watching you and we have to learn how to walk out our purpose because it's not just for us but it's assigned to bless others as well. You never know who needs to see you doing it so they know they can do it too. We give every reason under the sun as to why we can't do something instead of just trusting God.

Whatever dream God has put in your heart that you put on the back burner, walk it out in faith. Why? It empowers, encourages, influences and puts a fire under others. You have to walk out your purpose because somebody is watching you. Somebody needs to know they too were created for greatness. Stop making excuses and telling yourself that you can't do it. Stop allowing your lack of resources to paralyze you. When the vision is given by God, it automatically comes with His provision. We have a world to inspire and we are cheating somebody else the opportunity and the benefits to walk out in their purpose when we remain dormant. Some people just need to see you walk out in faith and that's enough faith to get them going. It's not that they didn't believe God the first time, but sometimes we allow our own insecurities, shortcomings and setbacks to stop us from doing the things we do need to do. If I didn't choose to walk in my purpose and do There's A Jewel In You anthology God's way, this young lady may not have been able to do what she needed to do for her purpose or it could have prolonged it even more for her.

Don't allow anyone to tell you who you are or what you can and cannot do. It doesn't matter if they think you're not qualified, because guess what, they have nothing to do with your qualifications. They have nothing to do with God's favor on your life. When He gives you something to do, stop trying to justify it to people who will never invest in you, who will never pray for you, who will never support you, and who will never encourage you. Just do it and do it God's way! In Mark 10, there is a story about a blind beggar named Bartimaeus who sat on the side of the road. When he heard that Jesus was walking by he cried out for help. The crowd around him told him to be quiet. Bartimaeus cried out louder and got Jesus' attention. When Jesus asked for him, the same crowd that told him to be quiet now is telling him to cheer up. Be watchful of people who are comfortable with you not living your purpose, but will cheer for you when it's your time.

Who is the crowd in your life that has told you that you couldn't go back to school? What crowd told you that you couldn't start that business? What crowd told you that you couldn't write that book? What crowd told you that you couldn't start that nonprofit, because you don't know anything? What crowd told you that you could not be successful? What crowd are you listening too? We have to be like blind Bartimaeus, and we have to cry out for what we want. People will try to box us in. They will make our circumstances determine where our future is going which just isn't true. Your past or present circumstances are not who you are. They are a part of you, but they do not define you. There is still greater in you that God wants to accomplish, but He's waiting for you to cry out even the louder. He's waiting for you to keep pressing forward. He's waiting for you to persevere. He's waiting for you to stop waving that old ugly white flag and to say by any means necessary, I'm going to be everything that God has designed and created me to be. Let me share something with you. If I had listened to the crowd, when I became a teen mom at the age of 15, you would not be reading this book. If I had listened to the crowd that looked at me in disgust, talked bad about me and said that I would be nothing but a baby maker, I would not be where I am today. The crowd does not have the power, authority nor permission to determine the outcome of your life. If blind Bartimaeus had listened to the crowd, do you think that he would be able to see again? He said, "Teacher, I want to see again." This tells me that once in life he was able to see, but something happened that caused him to go blind. Sometimes life happens. We make bad choices and things mess up. We are to learn from our mistakes and be better. Press pass the crowd so that you can get your breakthrough!

It's time for you to walk it out. There is a generation that needs to see that it's okay to be different. There's a generation of young people that needs to know that it's okay when you don't even know everything from A to Z to just go forth. Unless God tells you to sit down, you need to keep going. Stop confining yourself to your small circle. Position yourself around people who know how to think big. You want people who may say, "It looks impossible today, but God is still in control and you never know what can happen. The time is now. There's no better time than the present. If you see somebody who's trying to walk in their purpose and you know, somebody who tried and they gave up for whatever reason, encourage them. It doesn't cost you anything. Are you ready to walk in purpose?

How will you walk out your purpose?

Until you find your purpose,
others will find it for you.

~ CMW

There Is Still Room

Your oil is still flowing

There is a wonderful story in Genesis 26: 12-22 about how Isaac went and re-dug the wells by his father, Abraham. Every time he dug a well, the Philistines contended with him. They claimed rights to the well and the water. Isaac didn't fight with them. He would go dig another well and the Philistines would do the same thing. When he got to the third well and nobody quarreled with him, he named it Rehoboth, which means to make room. Had Isaac not preserved and kept digging, he wouldn't have known that room had already been prepared for him. What does that mean? Go dig up whatever you put down, because you were fearful of the opposition you faced. You didn't have the support or maybe you thought you were qualified enough.

Unless God has told you to leave it alone, go back and try it again because there is still room for you.

One of the things that Lord showed me that I missed when I read this passage before, the Philistines were not concerned about the wells until Isaac started redeeming them and found running water. Think about that. The Philistines were not concerned about the wells until Isaac dug them and found running water. Opposition only comes when you're trying to do something great. When you're trying to do something purposeful and make something of yourself, opposition comes. Does it come when you are just doing enough to get by or when you are living mediocre? Nine out of ten times opposition does not find you. Why? Because you're not attracting the attention of opposition. There are people who will come against you because they cannot benefit or take apart of what you're doing. Don't allow that to stop you. They can close 10 doors, but they cannot stop the 11th one from opening. Do you understand what I'm saying? People can come against you, but they cannot stop the oil from flowing in your life. The Philistines quarreled and contended with Isaac when he was re-digging those wells, but they never could stop the water from flowing. Why? God was the source of the water. Opposition is going to come, but don't get distracted by the opposition. Why? They cannot stop what God has for your life. They cannot stop His favor from flowing in your life. You have to keep digging. You have to keep moving forward. Why? Because it's not up to them. They don't control your destiny. They don't control your future. God does. When we wise up and realize who is over our life, we will start laughing at the opposition. The anointing attracts attacks. Don't get thrown off. Nobody passes a test by stopping in the middle of it. Don't allow the tricks of the enemy to make you grow faint and weary. No! Keep digging, keep pressing, and keep moving forward. That's the only way that you're going to understand that the water is still flowing. That the oil in your life is still there. You can do it. Don't worry about what you see in the natural. Rejoice about what you see and hear in the spiritual. There is still room for you!

Where will you go dig again?

Believe that you can and you will.

~ CMW

You Always Had Victory

Victory is not what you can do but what God has already done in you.

We already have the victory before the battle even started. We don't have to wish for victory. The victory has already been won. We just have to remind ourselves from time to time, I have the victory. When the devil tries to throw your past back in your face, tell him I have the victory. When the boss tries to keep you from getting a promotion, just say to yourself, I have the victory. When your enemies seem like they are increasing, remind yourself, I have the victory. When the doctor gives you a bad report, I have the victory. When your character is under attack and your integrity is being questioned and you know you haven't done anything wrong, I know it's hard, but to declare, I have the victory. You are ultimately saying,

> *Lord, however you give me the victory, I'm going to accept it. I put no limits on how the victory is going to manifest. I take my hands and my mouth off of it and I give it to you. Do it God for your glory. Do it so men can praise you. Do it so you can add to my testimony. Do it God!*

Many times, we're defeated because of our attitude, what we speak out of our mouth and also what we think. Sometimes we think ourselves out of the victory. Am I right? Have you ever had a time where you just were so overwhelmed and you were like, I don't know how this is going to work out and you kept those negative thoughts just rotating in your mind, looping, no matter how hard you tried, you can't think of anything positive about the situation? You thought yourself out of victory. How many of us has spoken negative words over a situation? This is just not going to work out in my favor. I'm just stuck. It's just going to happen and you allow others to join the pity party with you and so all of those negative words that were spoken, you spoke your victory right out the door. Even when you messed up and you're trying to fix it, the victory can still be yours.

No matter what situation that you're going through right now, no matter your circumstances, no matter what's coming against you, I want you to declare I have the victory! When those feelings of doubt and insecurity pop up, we have to cast down those negative thoughts and change how we speak. We don't allow anybody else to speak negative over us. Think about it. How many of us are stuck because we allowed somebody who we love or who we respected, to speak something negative and because they didn't speak anything positive, we automatically assumed it was over. I've been guilty too. Whenever you start facing that difficult, declare I have the victory! When you start feeling yourself reverting back to the old ways, you tell yourself, no ma'am, no sir, I have the victory. When the devil starts taunting and putting pressure on you, causing you to start to feel as if you are sinking, declare I have the victory. You speak yourself out of that thing until you get to the point where your faith is able to take you higher. Our words have the power of death and life. Choose to speak life as you walk in victory!

Where is your victory?

The promise is coming but if you move ahead of God, you may also create lifetime problems, which will impact how you enjoy your promise.

~ CMW

Who's In Your Situation Room?

Watch the security clearance you give to others.

There was a synagogue ruler, Jarvis, whose daughter was sick. He went to go get Jesus, when he got word that his daughter had died and they told him not to bother Jesus anymore. Jesus overheard the conversation and told him don't be afraid, but believe. They arrived at Jarvis' house and all of these professional mourners on the outside. Jesus told them she's not dead, but only sleeping. They went from crying to laughing in an instant. Jesus put them all out and took with him, James, Peter and John. If you know anything about the military, you know that the situation room is where life changing decisions are being made. You are handpicked and must go through security clearance. No one can walk up to the situation room and say, "Hey, I was just strolling by and thought I'd pop in." It doesn't work that way.

Our lives are like situation rooms and we should put people through security clearance before allowing into our lives. Not sometimes but all of the times. We have to stop allowing any and everybody in our lives when they have no purpose. They're just there to prey on us. They want classified information without the proper security clearance. Out of all the mourners that were on the outside of Jarvis' house, weeping for his daughter, none of them were cleared to go into the house to see Jesus perform His miracle. Think about how many people we allow in our situation room and give classified information. They have no intention of helping us or adding any real value to our lives. The type of people who don't have a word of encouragement when you're going through, but tell you to get over it. When they're going through, they want you to drop everything and come to their aid, but yet they don't have anything for you. You need to cut those people out. Kick them out of your situation room. We tend to keep a lot of people in our circle to feel confident and at times that hinders our breakthrough. God is saying, I can't do what I want to do with you because you have too many people in the situation room. We have allowed the enemy to creep in our lives, portraying as friends and now you're crying, "Why is this happening?" You got the wrong people in your inner circle. They're not sharpening you. They're not challenging you. They're not adding any value to their life. They really don't care about you, but yet you're giving them every bit of information about your life, your dreams, and what you feel God is wanting to do with you. They are secretly planning your demise. Yet we wonder why we've seen the same mountain for the last three, four, five, and ten years. It's time to downgrade security levels. This needs to be your declaration to them:

You no longer have clearance or have access to everything that's going on in my life. Because I realized our prematurely lets you in.

Sometimes we have to ask God to give us the strength to gracefully disconnect from some people. He will strategically move people out of your life. We cannot afford to let any, and everybody in just because they are good people with good hearts. There are good people. They may have a good heart, but they may not have any good intentions for you. It comes subtly. Take the time to reevaluate who you have allowed to come into your life. Ask yourself the following questions:

What value are they adding?

What is their purpose for my life?

Are they a distraction?

Are they making me better?

Are they pulling me towards God or away from Him?

Do they check me when I'm wrong?

Are they praying on me or preying on me? There is a difference.

Anytime somebody says, "I'm praying for you." You need to ask them, what specifically are you praying for and wait for their answer. If they have to a pause, that tells you, they're really not praying for you. That was just the thing to say. You need to make sure that they are not in your situation room. All of us at some point in time realized we have allowed people in our lives that should never be, or we've given people too much access because we've known them for a long time. Just because we're related, don't automatically give you access to my situation room. There will be times when we have those difficult conversations with people we love to tell them I love you, but you can no longer have access to this part of me. It doesn't mean you're a bad person, but you're not helping me.

I guarantee when you start analyzing the people that you have in your life and what they're actually doing to you and start moving some of those people out of the way, you can see God start to shift things in your life.

Everybody can't handle your blessings. Everybody can't handle where God is trying to take you. Everybody don't want to see you blessed. Let's be real. Some of us are connected to people that don't like us when God is elevating us. They secretly hope that doors were never opened for you. I hope you understand the importance of giving the proper security clearance for your situation room. The decision that are made in that room are indeed life changing.

What changes do you need to make to your situation room?

Divine timing is everything. Wait on it even though it seems like it is never coming.

~ CMW

You Are Not Forgotten

Your patience will determine your quality of life.

I know that sometimes as we are going through we can feel hopeless. We can get in despair. We can even think that God has forgotten about us. We see everybody else being blessed while living his or her best life. How many of you out there say, I'm anointed, but I don't have anything important to do? Sometimes that can be very frustrating especially when you know that you're called to a specific area. He heard your prayer the first time. He sees your tears. He knows that you're restless. However, we have to wait for his divine timing. What we do while we are waiting is what gets us in trouble. We don't like to wait because we live in this microwave society that says, I need it. I need it my way. One thing life is teaching me, it doesn't matter what He's doing in anybody else's life, because the plan that He has for my life has already been written in heaven. All I have to do is allow it to manifest in due time. Continue to wait on the Lord. Don't try to make things happen for yourself or get out of His will because you get antsy. We all get antsy. There are some things I get antsy about and I'm having to teach myself not to rush it because it's coming.

If we get it now, a lot of us will mishandle it. We would not do right by it. God has to allow some things to mature in us. We've got to purge some things out of us so that we can truly enjoy everything that He has for us. Beloved, God has not forgotten about you. You are the apple of His eye. You are always on His mind. He does not stop thinking about you. He does not stop caring for you. He will never stop loving you. He has not forgotten about you. Don't get into it to a mode of panic, where you start doing any and everything. Just continue to wait on Him because in due time, it is coming and you want to make sure that you're ready. You want to make sure that you handle it with the right attitude. Don't get upset. Don't get discouraged. Don't get in despair. He hasn't changed his mind about you.

I want you to think about David. He was anointed as King, but had to go back to tending sheep at his father's house. He didn't immediately rule the kingdom. He had to go back and serve. I ask you, those of you that know you're anointed to do a thing and yet you're still waiting on your time, how's your serving? Will you serve when nobody acknowledges you? Will you serve when you're overlooked? Will you serve why you're being mistreated? Will you serve when it doesn't seem popular? Will your anointed self still serve? David had to wait a very long time before he got the crown. He even had to go serve in the King's house to play the harp for him as evil spirits tormented him. He had to serve the man that he was going to replace. Now, how are you anointed for a position, then go serve the person that you're going to replace and do it in a humble spirit? Are able and willing to do that? We want the title, platform, and microphone, but what about serving? How is your attitude and motives? Are you consistent? Are you disciplined? Are you reliable? Are you dependable? Are you just doing it to buy time?

Before you can get to where you're supposed to be, there is a process. Unfortunately, many want to skip the process and go straight to the position. It's going through the process that builds your character and your faith. Are you able to serve while you're still anointed to lead? We know you can do XYZ and you can do it well, but until God says it's your time, what are you doing in the meantime? Are you willing to serve even when they are throwing daggers at you? Saul tried to kill David, but David still served him. How do you handle when you're being attacked by the one you're serving? Do you still serve in with humility? Do you still serve with purpose?

Sometimes we have to do a little self-check to remind ourselves, I still have to serve even though I'm anointed to lead. Don't think that your serving is disqualifying you from your anointing. It's not taking away from what you are created to do. It's actually adding to it. You have to change your perspective. Don't get so anxious to get there, that you don't build a firm foundation because it's the foundation you build while you're serving that's going to hold you up while you're anointed in that position. That's why you have to go through the process. Keep your eyes on Him and stay focused.

How has your impatience affected your life?

It's Already Yours

Being out of position blinds you from what's already in your hands.

Many people are praying, decreeing and declaring, Lord, I want this and Lord, I want that and Lord do this and Lord do that. He's saying it's already yours, but you're not in position. What does that mean? When was the last time you prayed and not one of those quick prayers? When was the last time you spent quality time in the word? When was the last time you fasted? I'm talking about a real fast, not this, Oh, I'm not going watch TV or I'm not going to be on social media. I'm talking about you turned that plate from 6:00 AM to 6:00 PM? When was the last time you asked God, what do you want me to do today?

When we compare our lives to others, it becomes more

difficult to recognize and enjoy the plethora of blessings in our own lives. You miss the fact that you really do have a great life. It doesn't mean everything's perfect. It doesn't mean you have everything that you want. You may be even deficient in some areas, but you remember you're still blessed. We live in a society that manipulates our emotions to feel insignificant if we don't have certain experiences or look a particular way. These fickle emotions cause us to miss out on what's already ours. We are more focused on what's not in our hands or what we don't have immediate access to. Now we have given the power to dictate our happiness to something that will always make sure we're not happy. The fear of missing out pushes us to always want more without being grateful for what's already been given.

We're crying to God saying, "God, I don't know why this is not happening." Have you followed the last instructions He gave you? I'll wait. I know. Me too. You're not in the boat by yourself. A lot of times the things that we're praying for and asking God to do, He's saying, I'm just waiting for you to get in the right position. We don't have to keep asking Him for the same thing over and over again because He's already answered the prayer. What position are you in? What position is your heart in? What position are your motives in? What position are your thoughts? What position are you in in order to receive everything that you're asking God for? The blessing already has your name on it. You don't have to name it and claim it. It's already yours. You just need to get in position. Are you going to be obedient to every single instruction and not straying to the left or to the right? Partial obedience is still disobedience. You can't declare that I'm blessed and highly favored and you're being disobedient.

In the book of Hebrews there is a scripture that says they did not enter into the rest because of their unbelief. It's referencing the children of Israel as they came out of Egypt. They were in the wilderness for 40 years because they were complaining, grumbling and murmuring. They had no faith. Some of us are the same way with so much doubt and unbelief going on in our lives. It blinds us from seeing the abundance that's already ours. The enemy doesn't have to attack us. Why? Because we're doing his job for him. We have doubt, unbelief and little faith in the ability of God. He doesn't have to show up, but still blame him because we don't have the things that we think that we should, or we don't feel God is moving in our lives the way we think He should be moving. We foolishly declare the enemy's just blocking and attacking me. No, he's not. Your lack of faith and your unbelief is holding up your blessings. It's already been assigned to you, but it's waiting to be delivered because of you. Thousands of Israelites died because of their unbelief. They did not see the promise land that was already theirs. What has died in your life because of your unbelief? What have you allowed to be buried in the graveyard because of your unbelief? Don't miss the promised land because of your unbelief. Stop complaining. Stop murmuring. Stop grumbling. Stop comparing your life to somebody else. Your life is not predicated on anybody else. What I do with my life doesn't dictate what God does in yours. No, it's all about where your faith is. What are you bold enough to believe God for? What are you confident enough to trust Him for? Speak over your life, "My parents may not have gotten it. My grandparents may not have gotten it, but I am the exception!"

Don't allow generational mistakes to stop you from moving forward. Don't allow generational curses to stop you from pursuing your dreams. Are you allowing what has happened in your family to tell you that you can't do it? That you're not going to succeed? That is nothing but a lie from the pits of hell. You are not what your ancestor did or did not do. You may look like them. You may have their same blood type. You may have similar DNA traits, but the quality of your life is not dependent upon what they did or did not do. You have to declare over yourself, "I am the exception!" Even if they cannot see it, you do it! Their lack of vision does not mean that it cannot be done. For whatever reason, God has put blinders on their eyes. Don't take their blinders and then put them on yours. You declare out of your own mouth:

I shall have everything that God says I can have. I shall be everything that God says I can be. I will do everything that God says I can do. Why? Because my purpose is already written in heaven. Even when it feels like it's not going to happen, I'm going to do it. Even when it's uncomfortable, hurts, or I cannot see what the end is going to be, I'm going to do it. Even when if I feel like I don't have anything to work with, I'm going to believe everything in me that I can do it.

The Bible says that His promises are yes and Amen. If He promised it, He's obligated Himself to it. You just need to make sure that God promised it to you. Don't take the promise of man and try to hold God accountable for it. God is not accountable for what man says or does. God is accountable for His word and His word only. He honors His word above His name. Find you a scripture and stand on it. Tell yourself, no matter what my ancestors could not do, I can do all things through Christ who strengthens me. I know my body is wrecking with pain, but I can do all things through Christ who strengthens me. I may be struggling, but I can do all things through Christ who strengthens me. With tears running down your face, declare I can do all things through

Christ who strengthens me. Ask Him to give you the strength, wisdom and courage to get in position. I ask you, "What has your unbelief caused you to miss out on what's already yours?"

Here's the good news because I don't want you to think because you had unbelief that it's over. As the old folks used to say in the old church, as long as you got blood running through your vein, there is still time to get it right. Give yourself a pep talk and say it's time to get it together. God doesn't bless sin and God doesn't bless mess. It would go against His character and His sovereignty. God is not looking for us to be perfect. He's looking for us to mature in this walk every single day. He knows we're gonna mess up. He knows we're going to have cycles in our life where we keep tripping over the same rock. He knows all of that. He doesn't change His mind about you. He doesn't change his mind about me. I was struggling with something for few days and when I hosted my first live event for women, I shared with a close friend how sometimes I think, "God, are you really using me to do this?" Without missing a beat, He says, "Chantea, My purpose for your life was already written in heaven before your birth. The mistakes that you're tripping over, I knew you were gonna make, but I didn't change My mind about you. Either you can stay stuck on those mistakes and be subpar or you can be exceptional. Accept my grace. Get in position."

I worked to get my thoughts and spirit in position before the event because this is what God has called me to do despite my mess ups, past, sins, and everything I've done wrong. Despite all of that, He called me for such a time as this. He's called you as well. Whatever purpose He has for your life, it's already written. It cannot be erased, but it can go unfulfilled if you don't get in position. Are you in position? Only you can answer that question. If you're not in position, what are you going to do to get in position? The choice is yours. God is not mad at you. He has not thrown you away. He is not like man. He loves you flaws and all. It is perfect for Him. Ask yourself, "What is one thing that I need to do today, to get in position? Start with that one thing. Don't overwhelm yourself with trying to fix everything at once. You didn't get this way overnight. It was a process. Getting back right is also a process. Give yourself grace. Stop being so hard on yourself. The only person that expects you to be perfect is you. Throw perfection out of the door. Get in position because the blessing is already yours.

You're only out of the race when you choose not to move.

~ CMW

What has your unbelief caused you to miss out on?

Will You Chase Your Purpose?

The graveyard is the biggest place of unfilled purpose.

In Luke 15, there is a story about a woman who lost one of her silver coins and it said she searched the house tirelessly until she found it. When reading this passage, I began to think, how that can apply to life and purpose. Some of us have lost our zeal and reason to go. Life happens. Situation happens. Some have been hitting brick road after brick road. It has caused you to give up. Some are just wandering through life wondering, what am I supposed to be doing? I thought I had it and I lost it. I don't know how to get it back. We all need to chase purpose like that woman who looked for her lost coin. Things are going happen in life that we have no control over. Some of those things happened because of situations that we started, or things that we did that we have not taken responsibility for, but you still have to chase purpose. Don't allow circumstances to cause you to lose your zeal. Don't allow what has happened to you, what people may say to you or how they treat you make you lose your zeal. It's imperative for you to chase purpose tirelessly because you will not have peace. You will not have joy. You will not feel complete until you are walking out your purpose. Everybody has a purpose. I don't care who you are. I don't care how dirty your past is. I don't care how mean you are. You still have a purpose in this life.

Purpose is just not going to fall in your lap or tap you on the shoulder and say, Hey, here I am. This is what you're supposed to be doing. No, you have to seek after it. You have to want that. You have to press through the storms of life. You have to climb up the mountains. What is stopping you from chasing your purpose? What cause you to lose your zeal? What causes you to lose your focus? What causes you to be distracted? What caused you to lose hope? What caused you to give up? Go back to the place when you were on fire for what it is you thought you were created to do and you said, this is it. I got it and then you got distracted. Life happened and you said, well, this must not be for me to do. What is it that makes us give up at the first sign of trouble? Those are things from the enemy to come to steal, kill and destroy your purpose. I want to remind you and me that we've got a responsibility to chase our purpose. Nobody is supposed to pump and prime you to walk in purpose. Nobody is supposed to manipulate or bribe you to walk in purpose. Nobody has to speak a word into your life or lay hands over you, to walk in purpose. It's an inside job. We have got to choose to chase our purpose. It's a choice. The question is, what choice are you going to make today? Are you going to make excuses or are you going to make moves? Are you going to make investments or are you going to be wasteful? The power's in your hands and in your mouth. We all have ups and downs. We all have things that we didn't expect or anticipate on happening. Instead of looking at it as a negative, flip it around and say, okay, how's this going to help me in my purpose? How can I use this to get forward? Don't just stay in a low place. Acknowledge it and then make a move with it. Stop making excuses. Will you search your purpose like the woman who lost her coin? She swept her whole house until she found it. Will you sweep your whole house until you find your purpose?

It's not supposed to be easy. It's not supposed to be a bed of roses. It's not supposed to be pretty every step of the way. They're supposed to be some struggle because it helps builds your character. It makes you honest. Somebody is waiting on you to chase purpose so they can know what they're supposed to do. Somebody is waiting on you to walk in purpose so that you can give them the missing puzzle link to their life. How long will you keep you waiting? The time is now to go forth. This is the day to walk in purpose. This is the day to search for it tirelessly. This is the day to say, you know what, come hell or high water, I'm going to do this thing. I'm going to make moves and not excuses. I'm going to make investments and not be wasteful.

When you start getting down, tell yourself, I don't have time for this. I'm chasing purpose. Don't let anybody tell you that you're not capable, that you're not experienced enough, and that you're not qualified. If He called you, He already qualified you. You may not have everything that you need today, but keep chasing purpose. As you chase purpose, you'll start to get the things that you need. He'll put people in your life to make deposits so that you are lacking no good thing. Don't give up. Don't wave the white flag. Don't lose your zeal. Chase purpose!

What caused you to lose your zeal?

You Are Graced For The Assignment

No matter what God has given you to do, you're already graced for it. We hit bumps in life and get discouraged. We feel like we're not going to make it. We make mistakes that we shouldn't have made. We've done things that we know we shouldn't have done. We feel like we've missed out on opportunities and it's not going to come back around again. We feel as if we may have missed our time. We tend to talk ourselves out of doing certain things because of the negativity and lack of self-confidence. We have to keep pressing forward. We have to keep telling ourselves I can do all things through Christ. It's going to get hard and frustrating. You're going to have days where you feel like giving up and throwing in the towel. You may even feel like what's the point of me doing all these things because it's just not working. You're going to have those days where you just don't feel like it. Whatever is going on in your life right now and no matter what the hardship is or what it looks like, I want to remind you that you're already **GRACED** for the assignment.

God has already anointed you for the places He's told you to go. He's already made the way. He did not say that it was going to be easy. He did not say that you would have the support you need from the people you think it should come from. Whatever He has told you to do, He has already empowered you to do it. Just don't give up. God, didn't give it to you because he wanted you to fail. He gave it to you because he can trust you. You think about that for a second. If He trusts us enough to give it to us, then at least we can do was complete it. Get up and get moving. Today is a good day to press that reset, but it's not too late. Pick yourself up, dry your eyes and keep it moving.

Sometimes we don't necessarily accomplish the goals that we set in our lives, or we stick to the resolutions that we make because we are go back to familiarity. We go back to what's comfortable. We go back to what we know. You DO NOT grow in your comfort zone. You must keep taking that leap of faith. You must keep doing things that may be unusual. You must keep doing things that stretch you. It's crucial to keep doing those things so that you can know exactly what it is that you can do. You're never going to know all of your capabilities when you choose to stay in your comfort zone. You have to get out of familiarity and go to a place that you've never been. You cannot be afraid. Stop looking back at what seems easy. Stop looking back at those things that aren't even challenging. You need to say, I believe enough in myself to take this chance. Who cares? If you take the leap of faith and you fall, at least you can say you did it. A lot of us aren't taking that leap of faith because we don't know what the end is going to be. We're fearful of the unknown. But let me tell you something. You don't know what the unknown is until you get to the unknown. It will stay unknown until you get there. Did you guys catch that the unknown is going to stay unknown unless you walk in it to know what it is.

If you remember the story of Lot's wife, as they were leaving Sodom and Gomorrah, she looked back and turned into a pillar of salt. Looking back causes you to be stagnant and not grow. A lot of us are not truly prospering and enjoying the abundant life that God has given us because we are looking back to what was and not looking forward to what's coming. You're wading in shallow waters and the deep is calling you. Just as God was with you in the shallow, He is with you in the deep. If you keep your focus on Him, He will lead and guide you. Everything is not going to be peachy. Everything is not going to be easy, but it is worth it. You think you've reached your milestone but you haven't capped out yet. There's more in you that needs to pour out.

You're going to make mistakes. Give yourself grace. You're going to make bad decisions. Give yourself grace. Everything is not going to go the way you have it planned. Give yourself grace. Stop being hard on yourself. Stop allowing other people to define you. You can still do it. I still see the best in you, but do you see the best in yourself? That's the struggle because we don't always see the best of us. Sometimes all we see is our blemishes, mistakes, faults, or imperfections. When you look in the mirror, tell yourself I am GRACED FOR THE ASSIGNMENT!

The burning question is, what are you going to do with that grace? Are you going to keep it moving or are you going to give up? Excuses are for people who don't want to do work and take a chance on them. People are waiting on you to show up. You are the answer to someone's prayer. You are unstoppable! Go and turn the world upside down!

What do you believe God has graced you to do?

About the Author

Chantea is a writer, speaker, and independent publisher. She is the ministry leader of Greater Working Women Ministries, where they strive to encourage, empower and equip women to be greater women. She is the owner of Relentless Publishing House, which serves Christian, inspirational and children book writers and assists them in self-publishing their books. She is also a chef and enjoys baking in her free time and for the holidays. As a former teen mother at the age of 15, her motto has become, "Giving Up Is Never An Option." She held on to Philippians 3:14 as her life verse and it has been her constant reminder when facing life's challenges. She firmly believes that every woman is GRACED to do something. Follow her on social media @GreaterWomen. To book her for your next event, email info@greaterwomen.com.

Additional Books by the Author

Greater Working Woman Devotional Volumes 1-3

Greater Working Woman Prayer Book Volume 1

I Am Still Somebody book series (for teen mothers)

20 Things I Learned As A Teen Mother (Kindle Only)

There's A Jewel In You Volumes 1-3 (Anthology)

Graced For It Prayer & Affirmation Journal

Are You Ready For Publishing?

Graced For It Devotional, Volume 1: Your Purpose Matters (Anthology)

Faith of Fear Prayer Journal

Get Your Write On Author Planner

Dear Single Woman (December 2020)

Lightning Source UK Ltd.
Milton Keynes UK
UKHW051614221020
371993UK00003BB/16/J